Confidence

D1565051

HBR Emotional Intelligence Series

How to be human at work

The HBR Emotional Intelligence Series features smart, essential reading on the human side of professional life from the pages of *Harvard Business Review*.

Authentic Leadership	Leadership Presence
Confidence	Mindful Listening
Dealing with Difficult People	Mindfulness
Empathy	Power and Impact
Focus	Purpose, Meaning, and Passion
Happiness	Resilience
Influence and Persuasion	Self-Awareness

Other books on emotional intelligence from *Harvard Business Review*:

HBR Everyday Emotional Intelligence

HBR Guide to Emotional Intelligence

HBR's 10 Must Reads on Emotional Intelligence

Confidence

HBR EMOTIONAL INTELLIGENCE SERIES

Harvard Business Review Press

Boston, Massachusetts

Copyright 2019 Harvard Business School Publishing Corporation
All rights reserved
Printed in the United States of America

10 9 8 7

Library of Congress Cataloging-in-Publication Data

Title: Confidence.
Other titles: Confidence (2019) | HBR emotional intelligence series.
Description: Boston, Massachusetts : Harvard Business Review Press, [2019] | Series: HBR emotional intelligence series | Includes index.
Identifiers: LCCN 2018044756 | ISBN 9781633696648 (pbk.)
Subjects: LCSH: Self-confidence. | Success in business—Psychological aspects. | Attitude (Psychology) | Emotional intelligence.
Classification: LCC BF575.S39 C66 2019 | DDC 155.2—dc23
LC record available at https://lccn.loc.gov/2018044756

ISBN: 978-1-63369-664-8

eISBN: 978-1-63369-665-5

The paper used in this publication meets the requirements of the American National Standard for Permanence of Paper for Publications and Documents in Libraries and Archives Z39.48-1992.

Contents

Contents

Contents

Confidence

HBR EMOTIONAL INTELLIGENCE SERIES

1

How to Build Confidence

By Amy Gallo

Very few people succeed in business without a degree of confidence. Yet everyone, from young people in their first real jobs to seasoned leaders in the upper ranks of organizations, have moments—or days, months, or even years—when they are unsure of their ability to tackle challenges. No one is immune to these bouts of insecurity at work, but they don't have to hold you back.

What the experts say

"Confidence equals security equals positive emotion equals better performance," says Tony Schwartz, the president and CEO of The Energy Project and the author of *Be Excellent at Anything: The Four Keys to Transforming the Way We Work and Live*. And yet he concedes that "insecurity plagues consciously or subconsciously every human being I've met." Overcoming this self-doubt starts with honestly assessing your abilities (and your shortcomings) and then getting comfortable enough to capitalize on (and correct) them, adds Deborah H. Gruenfeld, the Moghadam Family Professor of Leadership and Organizational Behavior and Codirector of the Executive Program for Women Leaders at Stanford Graduate School of Business. Here's how to do that and get into the virtuous cycle that Schwartz describes.

Prepare

Your piano teacher was right: Practice does make perfect. "The best way to build confidence in a given area is to invest energy in it and work hard at it," says Schwartz. Many people give up when they think they're not good at a particular job or task, assuming the exertion is fruitless. But Schwartz argues that deliberate practice will almost always trump natural aptitude. If you are unsure about your ability to do something—speak in front of a large audience, negotiate with a tough customer—start by trying out the skills in a safe setting. "Practice can be very useful and is highly recommended because, in addition to building confidence, it also tends to improve quality. Actually deliver the big presentation more than once before the due date. Do a dry run before opening a new store," says Gruenfeld. Even people who are confident in their abilities can become more so with better preparation.

Get out of your own way

Confident people aren't only willing to practice, they're also willing to acknowledge that they don't—and can't—know everything. "It's better to know when you need help than not," says Gruenfeld. "A certain degree of confidence—specifically, confidence in your ability to learn—is required to be willing to admit that you need guidance or support."

On the flip side, don't let modesty hold you back. People often get too wrapped up in what others will think to focus on what they have to offer, says Katie Orenstein, founder and director of The OpEd Project, a nonprofit that empowers women to influence public policy by submitting opinion pieces to newspapers. "When you realize your value to others, confidence is no longer about self-promotion," she explains. "In fact, *confidence* is no longer the right word. It's about purpose." Instead of agonizing about what others might think of you or your work, concentrate on the unique perspective you bring.

Get feedback when you need it

While you don't want to completely rely on others' opinions to boost your ego, validation can also be very effective in building confidence. Gruenfeld suggests asking someone who cares about your development as well as the quality of your performance to tell you what she thinks. Be sure to pick people whose feedback will be entirely truthful; Gruenfeld notes that when performance appraisals are only positive, we stop trusting them. And then use any genuinely positive commentary you get as a talisman.

Also remember that some people need more support than others, so don't be shy about asking for it. "The White House Project finds, for example, that many women need to be told they should run for office before deciding to do so. Men do not show this pattern of needing others' validation or encouragement," says Gruenfeld. It's okay if you need praise.

Take risks

Playing to your strengths is a smart tactic but not if it means you hesitate to take on new challenges. Many people don't know what they are capable of until they are truly tested. "Try things you don't think you can do. Failure can be very useful for building confidence," says Gruenfeld. Of course, this is often easier said than done. "It feels bad to not be good at something. There's a leap of faith with getting better at anything," says Schwartz. But don't assume you should feel good all the time. In fact, stressing yourself is the only way to grow. Enlisting help from others can make this easier. Gruenfeld recommends asking supervisors to let you experiment with new initiatives or skills when the stakes are relatively low and then to support you as you tackle those challenges.

Principles to remember

Do:

- Be honest with yourself about what you know and what you still need to learn

- Practice doing the things you are unsure about

- Embrace new opportunities to prove you can do difficult things

Don't:

- Focus excessively on whether or not you have the ability—think instead about the value you provide

- Hesitate to ask for external validation if you need it

- Worry about what others think—focus on yourself, not a theoretical and judgmental audience

Case study #1: Get the knowledge and get out of your own way

In 2010, Mark Angelo was asked by the CEO of Hospital for Special Surgery in New York to create and implement a program to improve quality and efficiency. Mark was relatively new to the organization. He had worked as a business fellow for the previous year but had recently taken on the role of director of operations and service lines. Even though he had background in operations strategy from his days as a management consultant, he was not familiar with the Lean/Six Sigma principles he'd need to use for this project and didn't feel equipped to build the program from scratch. He was particularly concerned he wouldn't be able to gain the necessary support from the hospital's physicians and nurses. What would they think of a young administrator with no hospital experience telling them how to improve quality and increase efficiency?

For five months, Mark struggled to get the project on track, and his confidence suffered. He knew that his apprehension was in part due to his lack of knowledge of Six Sigma. He read a number of books and articles on the subject, talked to consultants who specialized in it, and spoke with hospitals that had been successful in developing and implementing similar programs. This helped, but he realized he still didn't know if he would be able to get the necessary people on board. "I was anxious and stressed because I had no idea how I was going to transform the organization. I knew I couldn't do it on my own. It was going to take a collective effort that included our management team and all of our staff," he said.

He talked with the CEO, who had supported him since the beginning. He also looked to his family for emotional support. Through these conversations, he realized that his anxiety stemmed from a desire to be liked by his colleagues and therefore to avoid conflict. "After many discussions with my CEO and observing how he handled these situations, I learned that it is better to strive to be well-respected than well-liked," he said.

This was a turning point for Mark. Instead of worrying so much about what others thought of him, he focused on doing what was best for the patient and the institution. In December, he presented the vision for the program to the entire medical staff. While he was nervous about how it would be received, he knew this was a critical moment. "I was able to get up in front of one of our toughest constituencies and present the vision that we had been developing over the past few months," he says. His presentation was met with applause. "In the end, my confidence grew by leaps and bounds and we were able to design a program that has since taken off with great success across the hospital. I was able to overcome my mental blocks and knowledge deficits to build a program that will truly help transform how we approach performance improvement and patient care," he says.

Case study #2: Know the value you bring

Julie Zhuo knew she had things to say, but she wasn't sure how to get heard. As a product design manager at Facebook, she had developed valuable expertise in the products she worked on. Yet she lacked the confidence to share her ideas. She was used to being one of very few women in the room. That had been the case when she was studying computer science at Stanford, and it was still true now that she was at Facebook. She knew this meant she needed to make a concerted effort to speak up. But being the minority voice wasn't the only reason she felt unsure of herself. She says that she also suffered from "imposter syndrome," feeling as if she hadn't earned a right to her ideas—that she had somehow ended up where she was accidently, not through hard work.

Julie was intrigued when someone in HR told her about a workshop offered at Stanford by the OpEd Project. After attending and getting positive feedback about her ideas, Julie tried something she had never thought to do before: write an op-ed.

In November 2010, she published a piece in the *New York Times* entitled "Where Anonymity Breeds Contempt" about the danger of anonymity in online discussions. "It was a matter of someone saying 'You can do it,'" she explains. "It had never occurred to me that I could be published. But it actually wasn't hard at all." The reaction she got in the workshop and afterward back at Facebook boosted her confidence. Since then, she's gotten a lot of support from colleagues, which has emboldened her to speak her mind. "Of course it's still a work in progress, but now I'm a much more confident speaker and writer," she says.

AMY GALLO is a contributing editor at *Harvard Business Review* and the author of the *HBR Guide to Dealing with Conflict*. She writes and speaks about workplace dynamics. Follow her on Twitter @amyegallo.

Adapted from content posted on hbr.org,
April 29, 2011 (product #H0076H).

2

Overcome the Eight Barriers to Confidence

By Rosabeth Moss Kanter

To get a more confident you—or a more confident company, community, family, or team—first know what gets in the way. The best resolutions will go nowhere without the confidence to stick with them.

Confidence is an expectation of a positive outcome. It is not a personality trait; it is an assessment of a situation that sparks motivation. If you have confidence, you're motivated to put in the effort, to invest the time and resources, and to persist in reaching the goal. It's not confidence itself that produces success; it's the investment and the effort. Without enough confidence, it's too easy to give up prematurely or not get started at all. Hopelessness and despair prevent positive action.

To muster the confidence to work toward your goals, avoid these eight traps:

Self-defeating assumptions. You think you can't, so you don't. A British Olympic runner is so rattled by a misstep that cost her a contest that she dropped out of the next event. A company team decides that a popular world leader is so far out of their league that they don't invite him to speak at their customer event. Talented women sometimes "leave before they leave," as Sheryl Sandberg puts it, assuming that they won't be promoted (or succeed when they have children) so they start behaving like they're departing years before departure, thus foreclosing their options. It's one thing to be realistic, it's another to behave like a loser before entering the game.

Goals that are too big or too distant. I know how often leaders say they want to tackle BHAGs—"big hairy audacious goals." But having only enormous goals can actually undermine confidence. The gap between a giant goal and today's reality can be depressing and demotivating. Confidence comes from small wins that occur repeatedly, with each small step moving you closer to the big goal. But the small steps must be valued and turned into goals themselves. Winners think small as well as big.

Declaring victory too soon. This is the dieter's dilemma: You lose the first few pounds and feel so good that you reward yourself with chocolate cake—then when the pounds go back on, you feel so discouraged that you have more cake to feel better. I saw this pattern in a college football team that was coming off a nine-year losing streak (yes, nine years!). After winning its first game in nearly a decade, a team member shouted, "Now we'll win the championship!" First, of course, they had to win the next game—which they didn't. Step-by-step discipline builds confidence.

Do-it-yourself-ing. It's a trap to think you can go it alone, without a support system and without supporting others. Losing teams have stars, but they focus on their own records, not how well the whole team does; the resulting resentments and inequalities provoke internal battles that drag everyone down. To build your confidence, think about building the confidence of others and creating a culture in which everyone is more likely to succeed, whether through mentoring them or recognizing their strengths. Giving to others boosts happiness and self-esteem, as numerous research studies show. Supporting them makes it easier to ensure that they support you.

Blaming someone else. Confidence rests on taking responsibility for one's own behavior. Even in difficult circumstances, we have choices about how to respond to adversity. Whining about past harms reduces confidence about future possibilities. When the blame game is carried out within companies, everyone loses confidence, including external stakeholders. Confidence is the art of moving on.

Defensiveness. It's one thing to listen and respond to critics; it's another to answer them before they've done anything. Don't defend yourself if you're not being attacked. Apologize for your mistakes, but don't apologize for who or what you are. Instead, take pride in where you've come from and lead with your strengths.

Neglecting to anticipate setbacks. Confidence involves a dose of reality. It is not blind optimism, thinking that everything will be fine no matter what. Confidence stems from knowing that there will be mistakes, problems, and small losses en route to big wins. After all, even winning sports teams are often behind at some point in the game. Confidence grows when you look at what can go wrong, think through alternatives, and feel you are prepared for whatever might happen.

Overconfidence. Confidence is a sweet spot between despair and arrogance. Don't let confidence slip over into the arrogant end. Overconfidence is the bane of economies (e.g., the irrational exuberance that preceded the global financial crisis), corrupt leaders (who assume they're so necessary that they won't get into trouble for a small expense account fudge), or individuals who swagger and feel entitled to success rather than working for it. Arrogance and complacency lead to neglect of the basics, deaf ears to critics, and blindness to the forces of change—a trap for companies as well as individuals. Sure enough, like the old proverb, "Pride goeth before a fall," the slide into a losing streak often begins with a winning streak. A little humility goes a long way to moderate arrogance and keep just the right amount of confidence.

———————

Remember, it's not enough just to *feel* confident. You have to do the work. But with an expectation of success, you can try new things, form new partnerships, contribute to shared success, and revel in small wins that move you toward bigger goals.

ROSABETH MOSS KANTER is a professor at Harvard Business School and chair and director of the Harvard Advanced Leadership Initiative. Her latest book is *MOVE: How to Rebuild and Reinvent America's Infrastructure*. Follow her on Facebook and Twitter @RosabethKanter.

Adapted from content posted on hbr.org, January 3, 2014 (product #H00M4Q).

3

Everyone Suffers from Impostor Syndrome— Here's How to Handle It

By Andy Molinsky

One of the greatest barriers to moving outside your comfort zone is the fear that you're a poser, that you're not worthy, that you couldn't possibly be qualified to do whatever you're aiming to do. It's a fear that strikes many of us: *impostor syndrome.*

I know I've certainly had those thoughts while publishing pieces of writing, whether it's blogs or books. I've had them while teaching my first university classes and giving speeches to corporate audiences. I appear confident on the outside but feel deeply insecure on the inside, wondering who I am to be stepping up to this stage. What could I possibly have to say that anyone would want to hear?

And I'm not alone. Actress (and Harvard alum) Natalie Portman described the self-doubt she experienced as a Harvard student in a poignant commencement speech several years ago. "I felt like there had been some mistake," she said, "that I wasn't smart enough to be in this company, and that every time I opened my mouth I would have to prove that I wasn't just a dumb actress." Howard Schultz, the former executive chairman and CEO of Starbucks, revealed that he and CEOs he knows feel the same way: "Very few people, whether you've been in that job before or not, get into the seat and believe today that they are now qualified to be the CEO. They're not going to tell you that, but it's true."[1]

What can you do to overcome these feelings of inadequacy that so many of us experience?

A first tip is something that Portman highlights in her Harvard address, which I've found quite helpful: Recognize the benefits of being a novice. You might not realize it, but there are great benefits to being new in your field. When you are not steeped in the conventional wisdom of a given profession, you can ask questions that haven't been asked before or approach problems in ways others haven't thought of.

It's no surprise, for example, that some of the best research ideas I get as a professor come from undergraduate students with little previous experience, people who can think with a fresh outsider's perspective. This is true in business as well. The pharmaceutical company Eli Lilly has created a crowdsourcing platform called InnoCentive, through which outside innovators are paid to solve vexing problems the company faces. And it works! In fact, according to a study by Karim Lakhani of Harvard Business School, many problems are solved by those from outside the field in question—physicists solving chemistry problems, for example.[2] So the next time you feel inadequate in a particular domain, remember that as an outsider to the role in question, you might have the most critical perspective of all.

A second tip for combating impostor syndrome is to focus more on what you're learning than on how you're performing. According to psychologist Carol Dweck, the feelings that impostor syndrome leaves you with are ones we might actually be able to control.[3] With a *performance mindset*, which people suffering from impostor syndrome often have, you tend to see your feelings of inadequacy or the mistakes you make as evidence of your underlying limitations. This mindset only fuels the concerns you have about being unfit for your job. But there's something you can work to cultivate instead: a *learning mindset*. From this perspective, your limitations are experienced quite differently. Your mistakes are seen as an inevitable part of the learning process rather than as more evidence of your underlying failings.

That brings us to the third tip: Understand the power of perspective. Those of us who experience impostor syndrome often feel like we're the only ones feeling this way, but reality is very different. Early in my career, when I walked into a networking event, I was convinced that I was the only one worried about making small talk with strangers. But over time, I've realized that practically everyone in the room shares that same concern. According to a recent survey by Vantage Hill Partners, being found incompetent is the number-one fear of executives worldwide.[4] So if you're feeling like an impostor, chances are that others in your situation feel the exact same way. Or, as Tina Fey once quipped, "I've realized that almost everyone is a fraud, so I try not to feel too bad about it."[5]

It may not be easy, but overcoming impostor syndrome is possible—you don't need to feel helpless or alone. Next time you're in a situation that feels completely outside your comfort zone, don't focus on your failures. Consider it your opportunity to learn from your missteps and to bring forth a new perspective that others may not have.

ANDY MOLINSKY is a Professor of Organizational Behavior at the Brandeis International Business School. He's the author of *Global Dexterity: How to Adapt Your Behavior Across Cultures Without Losing Yourself in the Process* and *Reach: A New*

Strategy to Help You Step Outside Your Comfort Zone, Rise to the Challenge, and Build Confidence.

Notes

1. Howard Schultz, "Good C.E.O.'s Are Insecure (and Know It)," interview by Adam Bryant, *New York Times*, October 9, 2010.
2. Karim R. Lakhani et al., "The Value of Openness in Scientific Problem Solving," working paper 07-050 (Boston: Harvard Business School, 2007), http://www.hbs.edu/faculty/Publication%20Files/07-050.pdf.
3. Carol Dweck, "The Power of Believing That You Can Improve," filmed November 2014 in Norrköping, Sweden, TED talk, https://www.ted.com/talks/carol_dweck_the _power_of_believing_that_you_can_improve.
4. Roger Jones, "What CEOS Are Afraid Of," hbr.org, February 24, 2015, https://hbr.org/2015/02/what-ceos-are -afraid-of.
5. "Tina Fey—From Spoofer to Movie Stardom," *The Independent*, March 19, 2010, https://www.independent.co.uk/arts-entertainment/films/features/tina-fey-from-spoofer -to-movie-stardom-1923552.html.

Adapted from content posted on hbr.org,
July 7, 2016 (product #H02ZSC).

4

Mental Preparation Secrets of Top Athletes

An interview with Daniel McGinn
by Sarah Green Carmichael

Sarah Green Carmichael: *Welcome to the HBR IdeaCast from* Harvard Business Review. *I'm Sarah Green Carmichael. To get psyched up for the big game, sports teammates give each other pep talks, listen to an exciting song during warm-ups, or follow a particular pregame routine. Then there's a locker-room speech, often dramatized in popular movies, where the coach inspires individuals to greatness:*

[Excerpt from *Miracle*]:

Herb Brooks: I'm sick and tired of hearing about what a great hockey team the Soviets have. Screw them. This is your time. Now go out there and take it.

But what's the business equivalent of the pep talk? When you have a big presentation, job interview, quarter-ending sales meeting, or situation where you really need to be on, how do you prepare for it? If you're like a lot of people, you probably think about what you're going to say and what you're going to wear, and then you just kind of, well, show up.

HBR's senior editor Dan McGinn thinks we can all do better than that by taking a cue from how the best athletes and performers prepare. He's the author of the article "The Science of Pep Talks" in the July–August 2017 issue of Harvard Business Review, *and he is also the author of the book* Psyched Up: How the Science of Mental Preparation Can Help You Succeed. *Dan, thank you for joining us today.*

Daniel McGinn: Thank you, Sarah.

So did you have to get psyched up to write this book?

I did, actually. Writing this book did change the way I get ready to perform my job as a writer every morning or many mornings. If you watch sports, you become pretty accustomed to seeing the athletes and what they do when they warm up. They tend to have headphones on, and you know that they're listening to a certain set of songs. It's not just up to chance. You're used to seeing locker-room speeches. You're used to seeing that gaze, that locked-in look that they have, and that focus.

And they're taught to do that. There are sports psychologists who teach them exactly what they should be thinking about before a game. The argument I have is that more of our jobs are like that these days. It's less like factory work where you're doing the same thing every day and more about the big pitch, the presentation, the sales call, and that we should learn to do what these athletes do to try to lock ourselves in.

I think about coming into my job every day and that maybe we should run through the halls and give every editor a high five and then chew a pen and then put the pen back in the bin or other crazy things. How feasible is it to do some of these things on a daily basis?

Yeah, obviously, if our boss Adi Ignatius gave us a speech like Knute Rockne did before we sat down to edit articles, we would all think it was kind of crazy. If you don't know who that is, Rockne was the legendary Notre Dame football coach from the 1920s.

So why do people have rituals? And why is there a lot of research that suggests that they work? Well, one theory is that they help us remember how much practice we've done. They help get our bodies and our minds into the groove. The other is that they give us something to focus on other than being nervous and anxious. Think of a funeral. Funerals are very awkward occasions, and there's this whole set of rituals about what we do when we go through it. That's because it's awkward, and we want something to do to not think about the nervousness.

So there's a distractive element to rituals. They just help your body get into the groove. I'm not suggesting that we should run out and chest bump every day before we go to our desks. But I am saying that if you have some quiet, maybe private, thing that you do to get your day started, you might be a little bit better at it.

So a lot of what athletes and performers do is about reducing their pregame jitters. But isn't some amount of anxiety supposed to help you amp up for a big moment?

Yeah, no question. I was not a very good high school athlete. And when I started this reporting, I thought a lot of this was about adrenaline and about getting yourself psyched up, amped up, highly energized. The more research I did, the more I found out that that's really a simplistic view.

Adrenaline is a physiological response. But it's much more about what you're feeling, and it's about reducing your anxiety, trying to boost your confidence, and trying to manage your energy level so that it's appropriate to what you're trying to do. If you're a WWE wrestler, that's a little bit different than giving a commencement address. So you need to calibrate the energy level to make sure it's right for what you're doing.

What about trying to increase your confidence, though? I mean, can these rituals and things really help with that? Or is it like the movie Dumbo, *where little Dumbo had that silly feather and thought that's how he could fly? Is it just that this helps me because I believe it helps me?*

Yeah, so the feather would be an example of a superstitious ritual because clearly the feather doesn't really help him fly. It's just a placebo effect. What can help you gain confidence is controlling your thought patterns and thinking about what I'd call your "greatest hits." So, Sarah, for the show, if you were going to get yourself psyched up, you should think about the best podcast interviews you've done. You might actually want to go back for five minutes at your desk and listen to a couple of them.

Before I walked in the room with you today, I went back and listened to the best interview I've had with you because it made me think, "Gosh, you're good at this." And that's what you want to be thinking before you go into these environments. It sounds cheesy. You may remember the Stuart Smalley self-affirmations from *Saturday Night Live* in the '90s: "I'm special . . . People like me." But it does work. The messages there are to be relentlessly upbeat and positive. Be confident. Remember your greatest hits. And basically talk yourself up and psych yourself up with the idea that you've done this before, and you can do it again.

Was there any organization you came across where they really do make you go back and actually listen to or watch your greatest hits?

At the U.S. Military Academy at West Point, I spent a day in what they call the Center for Enhanced Performance, which is a team of psychologists that work at West Point. And one of the things they do is take their athletes and their cadets and put them in these enclosed, almost egg-shaped chairs. And they play audio tracks that they've created for each cadet that talk about how great they are.

The one I watched was a lacrosse goalie, and there's a professional actor narrating along with music: "John, you're the best lacrosse goalie ever.

Remember the game against Shrewsbury High when you did this?" So it really is a greatest-hits kind of thing. That's probably the most tangible, visceral example I have found of that.

Could it ever work so well that you'd get to a point where you were insanely overconfident and then that would actually lead you to perform worse?

Sure. I think in a sports setting or in a business setting, we certainly see examples of organizations that become overconfident, too convinced of their dominance, too complacent. But I think for your average, everyday business performers thinking about a job interview, a pitch scenario, a big presentation, or a negotiation, probably the average person suffers a little bit too much from a lack of confidence or an imposter syndrome. On the whole, most people are going to benefit from trying to dial it up a little bit.

One of the things in the book that really surprised me was the part where you explain that golfers who used Tiger Woods's clubs or clubs they were told were Tiger Woods's clubs—I'm not sure he participated in the study—actually golfed better than players who were just using any old random club. How does something like that work?

They call that process "social contagion," and it's the theory that knowing that someone celebrated or highly accomplished has touched an object physically imbues some magical powers. I tried to test that out in the book. I reached out to Malcolm Gladwell, who's a very well-known and acclaimed nonfiction writer. I asked him if I could write the book on a keyboard that he had used. Knowing that such a great writer has typed on these same keys and struggled through it absolutely helped me. I don't know if Tiger Woods's club would help

my golf game though. My golf game is really beyond help. [Laughter]

*Yes, I've actually read about similar studies—I'm not
sure how good they are—that show that when women
wear heels, they feel more confident. I think in my
case, the opposite is true, because I have a really hard
time walking in heels. But that's something where if
you are Stephen Colbert or David Ortiz or one of these
big stars you talk about in the book, you can really
control your environment so that you can perform the
ritual. But I think for most of us in offices, it feels like
we're not in control of our space. So how can those of
us who are not David Ortiz or Stephen Colbert really
carve out time for these rituals that are so powerful?*

They don't have to be super-elaborate, and they
don't have to be something that anyone else can
even recognize you're doing. So I don't do this

every day, but I'll put on a pair of noise-canceling headphones. That has a functional purpose because it blocks out noise, but also the feel of it on my head is a signal to myself that it's time to get to work here. Some of it is just this Pavlovian signal to our bodies that, "OK, it's time for me to get to work." So it doesn't need to be throwing chalk dust in the air or crazy hand gestures. It can be something as simple as putting something on.

DANIEL MCGINN is a senior editor at *Harvard Business Review* and the author of *Psyched Up: How the Science of Mental Preparation Can Help You Succeed.* Follow him on Twitter @danmcginn. SARAH GREEN CARMICHAEL was an executive editor at *Harvard Business Review.* Follow her on Twitter @skgreen.

Adapted from "Mental Preparation Secrets
of Top Athletes, Entertainers, and Surgeons" on
HBR IdeaCast (podcast), June 29, 2017.

5

Research: Learning a Little About Something Makes Us Overconfident

By Carmen Sanchez and David Dunning

As former baseball pitcher Vernon Law once put it, experience is a hard teacher because it gives the test first, and only then provides the lesson.

Perhaps this observation can explain the results of a survey sponsored by the Association of American Colleges & Universities. Among college students, 64% said they were well prepared to work in a team, 66% thought they had adequate critical thinking skills, and 65% said they were proficient in written communication. However, among employers who had recently hired college students, fewer than 40% agreed with any of those statements. The students thought they were much further along in the learning curve toward workplace success than their future employers did.[1]

Overconfidence among beginners

Our research focuses on overconfidence as people tackle new challenges and learn. To be a beginner is to be susceptible to undue optimism and confidence. Our work is devoted to exploring the exact shape and timeline of that overconfidence.

One common theory is that beginners start off overconfident. They start a new task or job as "unconscious incompetents," not knowing what they don't know. Their inevitable early mistakes and miscues prompt them to become conscious of their shortcomings.

Our work, however, suggests the opposite. Absolute beginners can be perfectly conscious and cautious about what they don't know; the unconscious incompetence is instead something they grow into. A little experience replaces their caution with a false sense of competence.

Specifically, our research focused on the common task of probabilistic learning in which people learn to read cues from the environment to predict some outcome.[2] For example, people must rely on multiple signals from the environment to predict which company's stock will rise, which applicant will do the best job, or which illness a patient is suffering from. These can be hard tasks—and even the most expert of experts will at times make the wrong prediction—but a decision is often essential in many settings.

In a laboratory study, we asked participants to imagine they were medical residents in a post-apocalyptic world that has been overrun by zombies. (We were confident that this would be a new scenario to all our participants, allowing them all to start as total novices.) Their job, over 60 repeated trials, was to review the symptoms of a patient, such as whether the patient had glossy eyes, an abscess, or brain inflammation, and diagnose whether the patient was healthy or infected with one of two zombie diseases. Participants needed to learn, by trial and error, which symptoms to rely on to identify zombie infections. Much as in a real-world medical diagnosis of a (non-zombie) condition, the symptoms were informative but fallible clues. There were certain symptoms that made one diagnosis more likely, but those symptoms were not always present. Other potential symptoms were simple red herrings. Participants diagnosed patients one at a time, receiving feedback after every diagnosis.

The beginner's bubble

We found that people slowly and gradually learned how to perform this task, though they found it quite challenging. Their performance incrementally improved with each patient.

Confidence, however, took quite a different journey. In each study, participants started out well-calibrated about how accurate their diagnoses would prove to be. They began thinking they were right 50% of the time, when their actual accuracy rate was 55%. However, after just a few patients, their confidence began skyrocketing, far ahead of any accuracy they achieved. Soon, participants estimated their accuracy rate was 73% when it had not hit even 60%. (See figure 1.)

It appears that Alexander Pope was right when he said that a little learning is a dangerous thing. In our studies, just a little learning was enough to make participants feel they had learned the task. After a few tries, they were as confident in their judgments as they were ever going to be throughout the entire experiment. They had, as we termed it, entered into a "beginner's bubble" of overconfidence.

FIGURE 1

Total novices lack confidence, but as their confidence grows, it outpaces accuracy

In a lab experiment, "doctors" quickly began to overestimate their diagnostic ability.

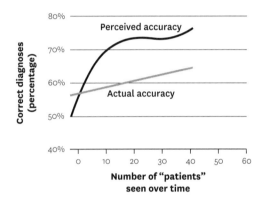

Source: "Overconfidence Among Beginners: Is a Little Learning a Dangerous Thing?" by Carmen Sanchez and David Dunning, *Journal of Personality and Social Psychology,* 2018.

What produced this quick inflation of confidence? In a follow-up study, we found that it arose because participants far too exuberantly formed quick, self-assured ideas about how to approach the medical diagnosis task based on only the slimmest amount of data. Small bits of data, however, are often filled with noise and misleading signs. It usually takes a large amount of data to strip away the chaos of the world, to finally see the worthwhile signal. However, classic research has shown that people do not have a feel for this fact.[3] They assume that every small sequence of data represents the world just as well as long sequences do.

But our studies suggested that people do eventually learn—somewhat. After participants formed their bubble, their overconfidence often leveled off and slightly declined. People soon learned that they had to correct their initial, frequently misguided theories, and they did. But after a correction phase, confidence began to rise again, with accuracy never rising enough to meet it. It is important to note that although we did not predict the second peak in confidence, it consistently appeared throughout all of our studies. (See figure 2.)

FIGURE 2

Overconfidence declines—slightly—with experience

But according to a lab experiment mimicking hospital visits, you can't keep it down for long.

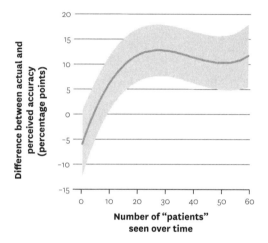

Source: "Overconfidence Among Beginners: Is a Little Learning a Dangerous Thing?" by Carmen Sanchez and David Dunning, *Journal of Personality and Social Psychology,* 2018.

A real-world bubble

The real world follows this pattern. Other research has found that doctors learning to do spinal surgery usually do not begin to make mistakes until their 15th iteration of the surgery.[4] Similarly, beginning pilots produce few accidents—but then their accident rate begins to rise until it peaks at about 800 flight hours, where it begins to drop again.[5]

We also found signs of the beginner's bubble outside of the laboratory. As with probabilistic learning, it has been shown that most people under the age of 18 have little knowledge of personal finance.[6] Most primary and secondary educational systems do not teach financial literacy. As such, personal finance is something most learn by trial and error.

We found echoes of our laboratory results across the life span in surveys on financial capability conducted by the Financial Industry Regulatory Authority.[7] Each survey comprised a nationally representative sample of 25,000 respondents who took a brief financial literacy test and reported how knowledgeable about personal finance they believed they were. Much like in the laboratory, both surveys showed that real financial literacy rose slowly, incrementally, and uniformly across age groups.

Self-confidence, however, surged between late adolescence and young adulthood, then leveled off among older respondents until late adulthood, where it began to rise again—a result perfectly consistent with our laboratory pattern.

It is important to note that our work has several limitations. In our experiments, participants received perfect feedback after each trial. In life, consistent feedback like this is often unavailable. Also, our tasks traced how confidence changed as people learned truly novel tasks. There are plenty of tasks people learn in which they can apply previous knowledge to the new task. We do not know how confidence would change in these situations. Relatedly, we cannot be certain what would happen to overconfidence after the 60th trial.

With that said, our studies suggest that the work of a beginner might be doubly hard. Of course, the beginner must struggle to learn—but the beginner must also guard against an illusion they have learned too quickly. Perhaps Alexander Pope suggested the best remedy for this beginner's bubble when he said that if a few shallow draughts of experience intoxicate the brain, the only cure was to continue drinking until we are sober again.

CARMEN SANCHEZ is a PhD candidate in Social and Personality Psychology at Cornell University. She studies how perceptions of abilities change as people learn, cultural differences in self-enhancement, and financial decision-making. DAVID DUNNING is a Professor of Psychology at the University of Michigan. His research focuses on the psychology of human misbelief, particularly false beliefs people hold about themselves.

Notes

1. Hart Research Associates, *Falling Short? College Learning and Career Success* (Washington, DC: Association of American Colleges and Universities, 2015), https://www.aacu.org/leap/public-opinion-research/2015-survey-results.
2. Carmen Sanchez and David Dunning, "Overconfidence Among Beginners: Is a Little Learning a Dangerous Thing?" *Journal of Personality and Social Psychology* 114, no. 1 (2018): 10–28.
3. Ibid.
4. Bawarjan Schatlo et al., "Unskilled Unawareness and the Learning Curve in Robotic Spine Surgery," *Acta Neurochirurgica*, 157, no. 10 (October 2015): 1819–1823.
5. William R. Knecht, "The 'Killing Zone' Revisited: Serial Nonlinearities Predict General Aviation Accident Rates from Pilot Total Flight Hours," *Accident Analysis & Prevention* 60 (November 2013): 50–56.
6. Stephen Avard et al., "The Financial Knowledge of College Freshmen," *College Student Journal* 39, no. 2 (June 2005): 321–339.
7. FINRA Investor Education Foundation, *Financial Capability in the United States 2016*, July 2016, http://www.usfinancialcapability.org/downloads/NFCS_2015_Report_Natl_Findings.pdf.

Adapted from content posted on hbr.org,
March 29, 2018 (product #H048R2).

6

To Ace Your Job Interview, Get into Character and Rehearse

By Cathy Salit

You've landed an interview for the job of your dreams. You're ideally suited for the position, and your resume is bulletproof. You've researched the company, the culture, the job, and the person who will be interviewing you. (Thank you, LinkedIn.) You've got your answers ready and selling points lined up. But when the interview starts, something's "off." You want to be commanding, but your nervousness gets in the way. Your voice sounds stiff. You hear yourself trying too hard, but you can't seem to stop yourself. As the minutes tick by, your answers sound more and more like canned monologues. And your interviewer isn't warming up—the job opportunity is slipping, slipping, slipping out of reach.

What went wrong?

As I see it, you probably prepared your content well, but—like many people—you didn't prepare something equally, if not more important: your *performance*. Yes, performance, the theatrical kind. Just as an actor prepares the character they will play on stage or screen, you can steal some tricks from the actor's toolbox to prepare the character you will play in the interview. For this kind of scene, you'll need to exude confidence, competence, likability, flexibility, and more. How to do this in a high-stakes situation? Tap into your natural ability to imagine and pretend—and craft your character.

"But wait a minute," you say. "Character? Pretend? What about being my authentic self?"

I get asked about that a lot, and it's a good question—many job coaches and experts extol authenticity, values-based behavior, and being "genuine" at work.

My company's own two decades of practice and research have focused on what we call the "Becoming Principle," in which the tools of theatrical performance give us the transformative power to become who we are not . . . yet. When we consciously use our capacity to pretend and perform, we can grow new—and genuine—parts of ourselves. (The Latin verb in the word pretend is *tendere*, literally to stretch, not to fake or wear a mask.) This idea resonates with the findings of Herminia Ibarra in her landmark HBR article, "The Authenticity Paradox." Ibarra writes that our adherence to one "true self" can hold us back as we take on new challenges and bigger roles. In other words, by sticking to "your story," you're limiting yourself.

In the job interview, you are literally *auditioning* for a new role. Developing your skills as a performer will help you not only to land the job, it will also help you grow and gain a new skill that is critical in the 21st-century workplace—navigating constant change that requires flexibility and new performances all the time.

Who do you want to be in this scene? That's where your "job interview character" comes in. Make a list of the qualities the successful candidate should convey. To some extent, these qualities will depend on the particular job you are applying for—a software engineer and a sales director will need to emphasize different leading attributes. And you'll want to convey in your performance that you have a feel for the company's culture—a laid-back dude vibe could be a turn-off in a formal environment, and vice versa.

Skilled interviewers will often be looking for the qualities that are known to correlate with success on the job, such as confidence, energy, and positive body language. How to physically act out these personal qualities? Much has been written about the body language of confidence and how specific gestures such as physical stance, tone, handshake, and eye contact instantly communicate both ease and authority. If you are not sure how to portray these qualities, look for others who seem to embody them, then observe, closely, how they do it. You're not looking to slavishly copy, but rather creatively imitate them. Try it on, try it out, and see what works for you.

Most important—rehearse! Like any good performer, you need to practice in advance. If you tend to be shy, expand your range of expression (and what you're comfortable doing) by practicing what might feel like an exaggerated performance, using hand gestures and passion. If you talk a lot using run-on sentences with no period at the end (a lot of us do this when we're nervous), practice pausing and breaking your thoughts into short sentences.

Even with practice and rehearsal, we can get overloaded and stressed in new situations, particularly when we're the center of attention and under scrutiny. That's why I suggest that—in addition to those outlined above—your job interview character have a special trait: Instead of performing as a person who is trying really hard to get the job, perform as someone who wants to have a *great conversation* with the human being across from you.

Your mindset is more like *I've done some cool and interesting things in my life and work that I'd love to share, and I'm really interested to hear about you and your company.* In other words, you'll play the role of a *good conversationalist.* Here's how:

- *Be curious.* Most people talk too much during an interview. Instead, perform curiosity—ask open-ended (not yes or no) questions that are connected to what you just heard. This will help you discover common ground with your interviewer, which is key to making a great first impression.

- *Accept every conversational offer.* Of course you need to prepare "talking points" for your interview. But being in a conversation (instead of delivering a rehearsed pitch) means creating back-and-forth repartee. That means you can do what improvisers do, and treat everything the interviewer says or does as an "offer"— which you should accept and build upon (rather than waiting for them to finish so that you can fire off another talking point). You can practice this kind of listening today, by starting every sentence with the words "yes, and . . . " Improv skills are now highly valued in the workplace. And in an interview, this fundamental improv technique will make you less focused on proving yourself and much more attuned to the other person.

- *Prepare to tell stories.* This may be one of the most powerful elements of a great conversationalist performance. The ancient art of storytelling has a powerful effect on stirring empathic emotions and boosting your own likeability. Prepare and practice yours in advance so that when the interviewer asks if you're experienced in leading projects, you can tell the story in a way that dramatizes the most recent project you led. Describe how the project began, what you did, the obstacles you faced and how you overcame them. Good stories have a beginning, middle, and end. Make them short, but pack a punch.

Some of these techniques won't feel like "you"—and that's the point. By making use of your natural ability to perform in new ways, you're expanding your comfort zone and increasing your repertoire of what feels natural. This is how you grow. It's how you become *who you are not yet*. It's also how you get the job.

CATHY SALIT is CEO of Performance of a Lifetime and the author of *Performance Breakthrough: A Radical Approach to Success at Work*.

Adapted from content posted on hbr.org,
April 21, 2017 (product #H03M6K).

7

Six Ways to Look More Confident During a Presentation

By Kasia Wezowski

Several years ago, colleagues and I were invited to predict the results of a startup pitch contest in Vienna, where 2,500 tech entrepreneurs were competing to win thousands of euros in funds. We observed the presentations, but rather than paying attention to the ideas the entrepreneurs were pitching, we were watching the body language and microexpressions of the judges as they listened.

We gave our prediction of who would win before the winners were announced and, as we and the audience soon learned, we were spot on. We had spoiled the surprise.

Two years later, we were invited back to the same event, but this time, instead of watching the judges, we observed the contestants. Our task was not to guess the winners, but to determine how presenters' nonverbal communication contributed to their success or failure.

We evaluated each would-be entrepreneur on a scale from 0 to 15. People scored points for each sign of positive, confident body language, such as smiling, maintaining eye contact, and persuasive gesturing. They lost points for each negative signal, such as fidgeting, stiff hand movements, and averted eyes. We found that contestants whose pitches were rated in the top eight by competition judges scored an average of 8.3 on our 15-point scale, while those who did not place in that top tier had an average score of 5.5. Positive body language was strongly correlated with more successful outcomes.

We've found similar correlations in the political realm. During the 2012 U.S. Presidential election, we conducted an online study in which 1,000 participants—both Democrats and Republicans—watched two-minute video clips featuring Barack Obama and Mitt Romney at campaign events delivering both neutral and emotional content. Webcams recorded the viewers' facial expressions, and our team analyzed them for six key emotions identified in psychology research: happy, surprised, afraid, disgusted, angry, and sad. We coded for the tenor of the emotion (positive or negative) and how strongly it seemed to be expressed. This analysis showed that Obama sparked stronger emotional responses and fewer negative ones. Even a significant number of Republicans—16%—reacted negatively to Romney. And when we analyzed the candidates' body language, we found that the president's resembled those of our pitch contest winners. He displayed primarily open, positive, confident positions congruent with his speech. Romney, by contrast, often gave out negative signals, diminishing his message with contradictory and distracting facial expressions and movement.

Of course, the election didn't hinge on body language. Nor did the results of the startup competition. But the right kinds of nonverbal communication did correlate with success.

How can you send out the same signals—and hopefully generate the same success? At the Center for Body Language, we've studied successful leaders across a range of fields and identified several positions which are indicators of effective, persuasive body language.

The box

Early in Bill Clinton's political career, he would punctuate his speeches with big, wide gestures that made him appear untrustworthy. To help him keep his body language under control, his advisers taught him to imagine a box in front of his chest and belly and contain his hand movements within it. Since then, "the Clinton box" has become a popular term in the field.

The box: Trustworthy, truthful

Source: Center for Body Language.

Holding the ball: Commanding, dominant

Source: Center for Body Language.

Holding the ball

Gesturing as if you were holding a basketball between your hands is an indicator of confidence and control, as if you almost literally have the facts at your fingertips. Steve Jobs frequently used this position in his speeches.

Pyramid hands: Self-assured, relaxed

Source: Center for Body Language.

Pyramid hands

When people are nervous, their hands often flit about and fidget. When they're confident, they are still. One way to accomplish that is to clasp both hands together in a relaxed pyramid. Many business executives employ this gesture, though beware of overuse or pairing it with domineering or arrogant facial expressions. The idea is to show you're relaxed, not smug.

Wide stance: Confident, in control

Source: Center for Body Language.

Wide stance

How people stand is a strong indicator of their mindset. When you stand in this strong and steady position, with your feet about a shoulder width apart, it signals that you feel in control.

Palms up: Honest, accepting

Source: Center for Body Language.

Palms up

This gesture indicates openness and honesty. Oprah makes strong use of this during her speeches. She is a powerful, influential figure, but also appears willing to connect sincerely with the people she is speaking to, be it one person or a crowd of thousands.

Palms down: Strong, assertive

Source: Center for Body Language.

Palms down

The opposite movement can be viewed positively too—as a sign of strength, authority and assertiveness. Barack Obama has often used it to calm a crowd right after moments of rousing oration.

The next time you give a presentation, try to have it recorded, then review the video with the sound off, watching only your body language. How did you stand and gesture? Did you use any of these positions? If not, think about how you might do so the next time you're in front of an audience, or even just speaking to your boss or a big client. Practice in front of a mirror, then with friends, until these positions feel natural.

Nonverbal communication won't necessarily make or break you as a leader, but it might help you achieve more successful outcomes.

KASIA WEZOWSKI is the founder of the Center for Body Language, the author of four books on the subject, and the producer and director of *Leap*, a documentary about the coaching profession.

Adapted from content posted on hbr.org,
April 6, 2017 (product #H03ETV).

8

You Don't Just Need One Leadership Voice—You Need Many

By Amy Jen Su

We often equate developing a leadership voice with finding ways to appear more confident. We assume that our success depends on mimicking someone else, increasing our self-promotion, or saying things more loudly than others. But rather than living with imposter's syndrome, or feeling exhausted by wearing your game face all day, you can build a truer confidence by more intentionally focusing on cultivating many different parts of your leadership voice each day. Ultimately, you should cultivate enough parts of your voice so that no matter the leadership situation or audience you find yourself facing, you can respond in an authentic, constructive, and effective way. So, what are the various voices to access within yourself and cultivate over time? And what are the situations that warrant each voice?

Your voice of character

First and foremost, consider the voice of your character. This is the part of your voice that is constant and consistent. It is grounded in fundamental principles about whom you choose to be and what guides and motivates your interactions with others. I've had leaders share that they hold key leadership principles in mind such as "Give the benefit of the doubt," "Don't take things personally," "Focus on what's best for the business," or "Be direct with respect" when walking into a difficult conversation, meeting, or potential conflict. Anchoring ourselves in the character we know we have keeps us from becoming chameleons, acting out of a fight-or-flight reaction, or only showing respect when there is a commercial gain or benefit—while being uncivil to others who we believe are of less value. A voice of character is ultimately about who you are and the intentions and motivations that guide your speech and actions.

Your voice of context

As you take on increasingly senior roles, your view and perspective of the business grow. You hold more of the big picture. Part of the job then becomes finding ways to express and communicate that bigger picture to others. Too often, in the race against time, we dive right into the details of a presentation, meeting, or conversation without taking an extra few minutes to appropriately set the stage and share critical context. Places where you can bring more of your voice of context include:

- Sharing vision, strategy, or upcoming organizational change with others

- Presenting to executives, and being clear on what you are there for and what you need

- Kicking off a meeting with your team and giving the bigger picture for the topic at hand

- Making your decision-making criteria or rationale transparent to others

Your voice of clarity

In a world of high-intensity workplaces, you have the opportunity to be the voice of clarity and help your team stay focused on the most important priorities. Leaders who envision new possibilities, muse aloud, or have knee-jerk reactions run the risk of teams trying to deliver on their every whim; these teams end up scattered, spread thin, and unfocused, falling short on delivering on the most important wins. Here are a few ways you can be the voice of clarity to help channel others' energies more productively:

- At the start of the year, sit down with each direct report to prioritize and clarify what the big wins are in each of their areas. One client of mine shared how she asks each team member: "If we were to publish this in a newspaper, what would you want the big headlines to be for you and your team at the end of the year?"

- Periodically come back to helping your direct reports reprioritize what's on their plates. You can do this in one-on-one meetings or with your entire team.

- Empower your team to say no.

Your voice of curiosity

As a leader, you have a responsibility to give direction, share information, and make important decisions. But you need to be sure that you're not approaching every situation as if you have all the answers or as if you need to advise on, problem-solve, or fix everything in front of you. In many cases, being the voice of curiosity is a better choice for the situation. As one of my clients once shared about facing pushback from others, "While I'm confident in my own business judgment and instincts, I know that my organization has hired really smart people. Therefore, if one of my peers or team members has a different perspective or pushes back, I don't take it personally. I get really curious to understand where they are coming from first so that we can get to the best solution." Some situations where bringing your voice of curiosity can help you and your colleagues move forward:

- When you're engaging in work that is inter-dependent, and a better solution will come from hearing all perspectives in the room before coming to a final decision

- When you're coaching a direct report, asking good questions to help them grow in new ways, explore issues they're facing, or support their career development

- When you're in a difficult conversation where hearing out the other person is an important part of defusing emotion, understanding each party's needs and views, and then figuring out the best way forward

Your voice of connection

As your span of control or influence grows, it can be-come increasingly more difficult to make a connection with a broadening set of colleagues, strategic networks, and teams. We often have folks working for us many layers deep into the organization, such that we no longer know everyone in our area and still must find ways to stay connected and visible. Being a voice of connection can come in many forms. Some of the ways I've seen others do this effectively:

- Increase your skill as a storyteller. Stories make our points more memorable and salient. They can enliven a keynote address or an all-hands meeting, drive home a point we're making in a presentation, or help to close a large deal or transaction.

- Thank and acknowledge. Our teams and colleagues often go to great lengths to ensure that deliverables are met, revenues are strong, and customers are satisfied. When we use our voice of connection, we remember to express gratitude to a team that worked through the holidays to close on the financials at the end of the quarter, or we remember to loop back with a colleague who made a valuable introduction or referral for us.

- Making time for a few minutes of icebreaking or rapport building at the start of a conversation or meeting. So often, we want to get right down to business, so we skip the niceties or pleasantries that help to build relationships with others. Where possible, and especially with colleagues who value that kind of connection, spend a couple of minutes to connect before diving into the work. On days where you're crunched for time, state that up front and transparently, so as not to create any misunderstandings. You can say something like: "I'm a little crunched for time today, so it would be great if we could dive right in."

———————————

Discovering and developing your voice as a leader is the work of a lifetime. The key is to stay open to an increasingly wide array of new situations and people. Use each situation as an opportunity to access more parts of your voice, rather than having a one-size-fits-all approach. Bring your voices of character, context, clarity, curiosity, and connection as the moment or situation warrants. Through this kind of learning and growth, not only will you increase your inner confidence and resilience, but you will also inspire the confidence of others around you in a more authentic and impactful way.

AMY JEN SU is a cofounder and managing partner of Paravis Partners, an executive coaching and leadership development firm. She is the author of the forthcoming book, *The Leader You Want to Be: Five Essential Principles for Bringing Out Your Best Self—Every Day*, and coauthor, with Muriel Maignan Wilkins, of *Own the Room: Discover Your Signature Voice to Master Your Leadership Presence*. Follow Amy on Twitter @amyjensu.

Adapted from content posted on hbr.org,
January 10, 2018 (product #H043HT).

9

Cultivate a Culture of Confidence

By Rosabeth Moss Kanter

One difference between winners and losers is how they handle losing.

Even for the best companies and most accomplished professionals, long track records of success are punctuated by slips, slides, and mini-turnarounds. Even the team that wins the game might make mistakes, fumble, and lag behind for part of it. That's why the ability to recover quickly and get back on course is so important.

Troubles are ubiquitous. Surprises can fall from the sky like volcanic ash and appear to change everything. New ventures can begin with great promise and still face unexpected obstacles, unanticipated delays, and critics that pop up at the wrong moment. That's why I coined Kanter's Law: "Anything can look like a failure in the middle."

Nothing succeeds for long without considerable effort and constant vigilance. Winning streaks end for predictable reasons: Strategies run their course. New competition emerges to take on the industry leader. Ideas get dusty. Technology marches on. Complacency sets in, making people feel entitled to success rather than motivated to work for it.

Thus, a key factor in high achievement is bouncing back from the low points. Long-term winners often face the same problems as long-term losers, but they respond differently, as I found in the research for my book *Confidence*. I compared companies and sports teams with long winning streaks and long losing streaks, and then looked at how leaders led turnarounds from low to high performance.

Consider first the pathologies of losing. Losing produces temptations to behave in ways that make it hard to recover fast enough—and could even make the situation worse. For example, panicking and throwing out the game plan. Scrambling for self-protection and abandoning the rest of the group. Hiding the facts and hoping that things will get better by themselves before anyone notices. Denying that there is anything to learn or change. Using decline as an excuse to let facilities or investments deteriorate.

The culture and support system that surrounds high performers helps them avoid these temptations. They can put troubles in perspective because they are ready for them. They rehearse through diligent practice and preparation; they remain disciplined and professional. Their leaders put facts on the table and review what went right or wrong in the last round in order to shore up strengths and pinpoint weaknesses and to encourage personal responsibility for actions. They stress collaboration and teamwork—common goals; commitment to a joint vision; respect and support for team members, so when someone drops the ball, someone else is there to pick it up—and responsibility for mentoring, so the best performers lift everyone's capabilities. They seek creative ideas for improvement and innovation, favoring widespread dialogue and brainstorming.

Resilience is not simply an individual characteristic or a psychological phenomenon. It is helped or hindered by the surrounding system. Teams that are immersed in a culture of accountability, collaboration, and initiative are more likely to believe that they can weather any storm. Self-confidence, combined with confidence in one another and in the organization, motivates winners to make the extra push that can provide the margin of victory.

The lesson for leaders is clear: Build the cornerstones of confidence—accountability, collaboration, and initiative—when times are good and achievement comes easily. Maintain a culture of confidence as insurance against the inevitable downturns. And while no one should deliberately seek failure, remember that performance under pressure—the ability to stay calm, learn, adapt, and keep on going—separates winners from losers.

ROSABETH MOSS KANTER is a professor at Harvard Business School and chair and director of the Harvard Advanced Leadership Initiative. Her latest book is *MOVE: How to Rebuild and Reinvent America's Infrastructure*. Follow her on Facebook and Twitter @RosabethKanter.

Reprinted from *Harvard Business Review*,
April 2011 (product #F1104E).

10

Great Leaders Are Confident, Connected, Committed, and Courageous

By Peter Bregman

B rad was leading a difficult turnaround of his company and had decided to fire his head of sales, who was a nice guy but wasn't performing. Three months later, he still hadn't fired him.

I asked him why. His answer? "I'm a wimp!"

Brad (not his real name—I've changed some details to protect people's privacy) is the CEO of a financial services firm and is most definitely not a wimp. He's a normal human, just like you and me. And he's struggling to follow through on an important, strategic decision. Just like, at times, you and I do.

No matter your age, your role, your position, your title, your profession, or your status, to get your most important work done, you have to have hard conversations, create accountability, and inspire action.

In order to do that, you need to show up powerfully and magnetically in a way that attracts people to trust you, follow you, and commit to putting 100% of their effort into a larger purpose, something bigger than all of you. You need to care about others and connect with them in such a way that they feel your care. You need to speak persuasively—in a way that's clear, direct, and honest and that reflects your care— while listening with openness, compassion, and love. Even when being challenged.

And, of course, you need to follow through quickly and effectively.

In 25 years of working with leaders to do all of the above, I have found a pattern that I share in my book, *Leading with Emotional Courage*, consisting of four essential elements that all great leaders rely on to rally people to accomplish what's important to them. To lead effectively—really, to *live* effectively—you must be confident in yourself, connected to others, committed to purpose, and emotionally courageous.

Most of us are great at only one of the four. Maybe two. But to be a powerful presence—to inspire action—you need to excel at *all four simultaneously*.

If you're confident in yourself but disconnected from others, everything will be about you and you'll alienate the people around you. If you're connected to others but lack confidence in yourself, you will betray your own needs and perspectives in order to please everyone else. If you're not committed to a purpose, something bigger than yourself and others, you'll flounder, losing the respect of those around you as you act aimlessly, failing to make an impact on what matters most. And if you fail to act powerfully, decisively, and boldly—with emotional courage—your ideas will remain idle thoughts and your goals will remain unfulfilled fantasies.

Let's apply this to Brad and identify precisely where and how he was getting stuck.

Confident in yourself

Brad struggled with this element, which might feel surprising since he was so successful in his career. But this is not uncommon. He worked tremendously hard, but it came from some degree of insecurity— he wanted to prove himself and please those around him. He became unnerved in the face of potential failure and was not particularly gentle or compassionate with himself when he did fail. He did have important strengths in this element: He saw the person he wanted to become and he worked toward that future, putting aside distractions and investing his energy wisely and strategically.

Connected to others

This was Brad's greatest strength. He was well-loved and always took great care of his team. People clearly knew and felt that he trusted them, even when he disagreed with them. They appreciated his curiosity—

about people and problems—and were grateful that he did not draw quick conclusions about them. All that said, even in this element, he had room to grow: He was not always direct with people and tended to procrastinate on difficult conversations.

Committed to purpose

This was a mixed element for Brad. On the one hand, Brad was clear about what needed to get done to grow the firm, he engaged people in the early stages of work, and he was open and willing to ask for help. On the other hand, he was somewhat scattered. He wasn't clear enough about the small number of things that would move the needle, and he didn't have a reliable process for staying focused on the most important things, ensuring accountability and driving follow-through. Not firing his head of sales sent a mixed message to his team—was he really serious about the firm's success?

Emotionally courageous

Brad had room to grow here, and it turned out to be an important element for growing his strength in the other three elements. Risks, by definition, make us feel vulnerable, and Brad avoided that feeling. He resisted the unknown and intentionally avoided uncomfortable situations. This made it hard for him to tell people hard truths and make hard decisions quickly, which stalled his actions.

So Brad's strongest element was "connected to others," followed by "committed to purpose." He was weaker in "confident in yourself" and "emotionally courageous."

Which puts his challenge in perspective: His connection to his head of sales was at war with his commitment to the success of his team and company. Meanwhile, his confidence in himself and his emotional courage weren't strong enough to break the tie. That's a recipe for inaction and painful frustration.

Just knowing what was happening helped him immediately. We spent some time strengthening his emotional courage by taking small risks *while* feeling the emotions he had been trying to keep at bay. Each time he followed through, regardless of whether he succeeded, he obviously survived and also felt the accomplishment of addressing the risk itself. Which, of course, built his confidence. Which helped him take bigger risks.

In a short time, he felt prepared (even though he may never have felt "ready") to follow through on what he had known he needed to do for the past three months. With his natural care, compassion, and humanity, he fired his head of sales (who, by the way, and unsurprisingly, knew it was coming and said he felt "relieved").

Brad was extremely uncomfortable going into the conversation—that's almost always the feeling you'll have when you do anything that requires emotional courage.

But using emotional courage builds your emotional courage. Brad emerged from the conversation stronger in all four elements: He was more confident in himself, more connected to his team (and even, believe it or not, his head of sales), more committed to purpose, and more emotionally courageous.

PETER BREGMAN is CEO of Bregman Partners, a company that helps senior leaders create accountability and inspire collective action on their organization's most important work. He is the best-selling author of *18 Minutes*, and his latest book is *Leading with Emotional Courage*. He is also the host of the Bregman Leadership Podcast.

Adapted from content posted on hbr.org,
July 13, 2018 (product #H04FUI).

11

Helping an Employee Overcome Their Self-Doubt

By Tara Sophia Mohr

*Y*ou want to give a member of your team a stretch assignment, but she tells you she's just "not ready yet"—she'd like to get more experience before taking it on.

You offer to make a valuable introduction for someone you mentor. He seems excited about it at first, but doesn't follow up. Later, you discover that he felt intimidated, like he'd have nothing to say.

As managers and mentors, we frequently encounter situations like these, when we come up against the limiting voices of self-doubt in the people we support.

The negative impact of that voice is tremendous. If someone on your team is hampered by a harsh inner critic, they're likely to talk themselves out of sharing their ideas and insights. Held back by self-doubt, some of your most talented people will shy away from leading projects or teams, or put off going for the big opportunities—new clients, new business lines, innovative moves—that could help your business grow.

As a manager or mentor, one of the most powerful ways you can unlock your people's potential is to give them a tool kit for managing self-doubt.

The manager's common mistake

Typically, managers and mentors make this mistake: They think their job is to encourage, compliment, or cheerlead when their people are struggling with self-doubt. They say things like, "You really *can* do this!" or "I have complete confidence in you. I wouldn't have given you this role if I didn't think you had the capability to do it."

In the coaching field, this is known as "arguing with the inner critic." It's the dialogue between someone's voice of self-doubt (*"I can't do that, I don't have what it takes, etc."*) and the affirming words of a supportive person who has a different perspective (*"Yes you can! You are great!"*).

Coaches-in-training are taught, "Never, never argue with the client's inner critic." It's understood that such arguments are usually a waste of everyone's time, for two reasons.

First, such reassurance rarely is convincing. The inner critic's view is not based in data but in instinctual, over-reactive fears of vulnerability and failure. Hearing another individual say something along the lines of "No, you're great at that!" often doesn't speak to those underlying fears. In fact, it can *add* to the stressful feelings of being an imposter, as in, "No one around me realizes that I *really* don't know what I'm doing, and they are all counting on me, thinking I can pull this off—but I can't!"

Second, if you help team members and mentees through their self-doubt by giving them compliments or reassurances, the solution requires your presence or the presence of someone like you. You're giving your people fish, but you aren't teaching them *how* to fish. You haven't given them tools to navigate self-doubt on their own. That's what they really need, because they will make most of their inner-critic-driven decisions quickly, in their own heads, without talking to anyone.

An alternative approach

The alternative is to take the conversation up a level. Instead of arguing with your team members' inner critics, you can introduce a conversation *about* self-doubt—what it is, why it shows up for each of us, and how it can impact what you achieve as a team. You can start to do this with a couple of steps.

1. *Introduce the idea of the "inner critic."* You might choose to call it imposter syndrome, the voice of self-doubt, monkey mind, or another term you feel is appropriate for your work context.

   What's key is to introduce the concept of a voice in all of our heads that does not reflect realistic thinking, and that anxiously and irrationally underestimates our own capabilities. There are common qualities of the inner critic's voice you can use to help your people identify their critics: a voice that critiques harshly, is irrational or untrue, sounds like a broken record, or makes arguments about what's in your best interest, for instance.[1] You can also use the table "Get to know your inner critic" to talk about the difference between the inner critic and more realistic thinking.

2. *Ask your team members to start developing the skill of managing their inner critics.* Clarify

Get to know your inner critic

How the voice in your head compares with realistic thinking.

Inner critic	Realistic thinking
• Very sure it knows the truth of the situation	• Curious and conscious of the many unknowns in the situation
• Asks yes/no questions: *"Is it possible?"*	• Asks open-ended questions: *"How might this be possible?" "What part is possible?"*
• Focuses on problems	• Seeks solutions
• Sounds anxious and pessimistic in tone	• Sounds calmer and generative in tone
• Thinks in extreme, black-and-white terms	• Able to see subtlety and gray
• Is repetitive	• Is forward-moving

that you understand that fears and self-doubts will naturally come up when your team members or mentees grow into new roles, take on greater responsibility, or speak up. The goal you want them to work toward is not unfailing confidence but more-skillful management of their own limiting beliefs and self-doubts.

In doing this, you are introducing a powerful new idea: that readiness for advancement and leadership does not depend on an innate quality of confidence but rather on building the skill of managing one's own self-doubts.

To do this, they should practice noticing when they're hearing their critic, and to name the critic's thoughts as such when they occur. That's as simple as noting to oneself, "I'm hearing my inner critic's worries about this again."

Typically, once someone understands the fear-based roots of the critic's voice and is conscious of when it's speaking up, they can choose to not take direction from it and to take direction from more resourceful and rational parts of themselves instead.

One woman in my course, a manager at a telecommunications company, brought a small group of her colleagues together for this conversation. One colleague told her afterward, "I knew I had a little, mean, nagging voice inside my head, but until now I hadn't really appreciated how much impact it had on the choices I make." Another realized she was not applying for an available promotion largely because of her inner critic. After the discussion, she applied for the job—and got it.

Grace, an executive at a professional services firm, worked with a manager who was dealing with major changes in the scope of her role, activating the manager's inner critic. "In addition to encouraging her," Grace said, "we spent time digging through how the changes had triggered her inner critic. We made a clear plan for what she needed to accomplish. Many milestones were reached (and celebrated), but when things didn't go to plan, we explored whether/how the manager's inner critic was factoring in. As time went on, the manager learned to better predict when her inner critic might kick in and how it could be quieted. She gained a tool she can rely on and navigated challenging times of change with flying colors."

You want your people to do all that they are capable of—to keep saying "yes" to being on their growing edge. That means they'll frequently feel self-doubt.

You can empower them by addressing the inner critic head-on, and you can give them tools to become skillful responders to their own self-doubt.

TARA SOPHIA MOHR is an expert on women's leadership and the author of *Playing Big: Practical Wisdom for Women Who Want to Speak Up, Create, and Lead*, named a best book of the year by Apple's iBooks. She is the creator of the Playing Big leadership programs for women, which now have more than 2,000 graduates worldwide. Connect with her at taramohr.com.

Note

1. Tara Mohr, "7 Ways to Recognize Your Inner Critic," https://www.taramohr.com/inspiration/7-ways-to -recognize-your-inner-critic/.

Adapted from content posted on hbr.org,
October 1, 2015 (product #H02DB8).

12

To Seem Confident, Women Have to Be Seen as Warm

By Margarita Mayo

Why are there so few women in leadership roles? My research collaborators (Laura Guillén of ESMT and Natalia Karelaia of INSEAD) and I believe we have shed some new light on this conundrum. But first, some background.

One frequently cited reason has to do with confidence. In a previous study, my colleagues and I found that women tend to rate their abilities accurately, while men tend to be overconfident about theirs.[1] Thus, one argument goes, women are less confident than men, which hurts their chances of promotion.

Previous research has measured how women see themselves, but we wanted to know how outside perceivers—bosses, subordinates, colleagues—rate women's confidence, and what influences those ratings.

Susan Fiske and her colleagues have shown that people seem to universally use two dimensions to judge others: competence and warmth.[2] We decided to test for both of those in addition to confidence. As a proxy for the likelihood of being promoted, we also tested for influence, on the theory that people who are seen as influential are more likely to be promoted to leadership roles.

We conducted a study analyzing the judgments that colleagues made regarding the competence and warmth of 236 engineers working in project teams at a multinational software development company.[3] As part of their performance evaluation, the engineers were evaluated online by their supervisor, peers, and collaborators on competence and warmth. A total of 810 raters provided this confidential evaluation. A year later, we collected a second wave of data on the same 236 engineers about their apparent confidence at work and their influence in the organization. This time, a total of 1,236 raters provided information.

Our study shows that men are seen as confident if they are seen as competent, but women are seen as confident only if they come across as both competent and warm. Women must be seen as warm in order to capitalize on their competence and be seen as confident and influential at work; competent men are seen as confident and influential whether they are warm or not.

In other words, for male engineers, competence and perceived confidence go hand in hand. The more competent male engineers are, the more confident they are seen as being (and vice versa). The more confident they are seen as being, the more influence they have in the organization, regardless of whether others like them. It seems that warmth is irrelevant to men appearing confident and influential, at least when they are performing a typically male job like engineering.

For women, in the absence of warmth there was virtually no relationship between competence and confidence ratings. When women were seen as both warm and competent, they were also seen as more confident—and thus more influential. Competent but less-affable female engineers were evaluated by their colleagues as less confident in their professional roles. These female engineers were, in turn, less influential within the organization. In sum, women's professional performance is not evaluated independently from their personal warmth.

Personal experience and empirical research suggest that it's not enough for women to be merely *as* gregarious, easygoing, sociable, and helpful as men. To get credit for being warm—and to have their other strengths recognized—they might need to be even more so.

I still remember my first performance evaluation as an assistant lecturer: I was told to be more "nurturing." I had gone to just as many social events as the men had, had been just as gregarious with my students. But women simply are expected to show more warmth. Studies show, for example, that women's performance reviews contain nearly twice as much language about being warm, empathetic, helpful, and dedicated to others.[4]

To us, this study suggests that if women are to succeed in a biased world, encouraging them to be more confident is not enough. To get credit for having confidence and competence, and to have the influence in their organizations that they would like to have, women must go out of their way to be seen as warm.

We wish this were not the case. We wish women and men could be evaluated according to the same meritocratic standards. But as our research shows, we seem to be a long way off from those days.

MARGARITA MAYO is Professor of Leadership and Organizational Behavior at IE Business School in Madrid. She was featured on the Thinkers50 Radar as one of 30 thought leaders to watch in 2017. She is the author of *Yours Truly: Staying Authentic in Leadership and Life*.

Notes

1. Margarita Mayo et al., "Aligning or Inflating Your Leadership Self-Image? A Longitudinal Study of Responses to Peer Feedback in MBA Teams," *Academy of Management Learning and Education* 11, no. 4 (2012): 631–652.
2. Susan T. Fiske et al., "Universal Dimensions of Social Cognition: Warmth and Competence," *Trends in Cognitive Sciences* 11, no. 2 (2006): 77–83.
3. Laura Guillén et al., "The Competence-Confidence Gender Gap: Being Competent Is Not Always Enough for Women to Appear Confident," working paper (Berlin: ESMT, 2016), https://margaritamayo.com/wp-content/uploads/2016/07/The-competence-confidence-gender-gap.pdf.
4. Shelley Correll and Caroline Simard, "Research: Vague Feedback Is Holding Women Back," hbr.org, April 29, 2016, https://hbr.org/2016/04/research-vague-feedback-is-holding-women-back.

Adapted from content posted on hbr.org,
July 8, 2016 (product #H03036).

13

Why Do So Many Incompetent Men Become Leaders?

By Tomas Chamorro-Premuzic

There are three popular explanations for the clear underrepresentation of women in management: They are not capable; they are not interested; or they are both interested and capable, but they are unable to break the glass ceiling, an invisible career barrier based on prejudiced stereotypes that prevents women from accessing the ranks of power. Conservatives and chauvinists tend to endorse the first; liberals and feminists prefer the third; and those somewhere in the middle are usually drawn to the second. But what if they have all missed the big picture?

In my view, the main reason for the unbalanced gender ratio in management is our inability to discern between confidence and competence. That is, because we (people in general) commonly misinterpret displays of confidence as a sign of competence, we are fooled into believing that men are better leaders than women. In other words, when it comes to leadership, the only advantage that men have over women (from Argentina to Norway and the USA to Japan) is the fact that manifestations of hubris—often masked as charisma or charm—are commonly mistaken for leadership potential and that these occur much more frequently in men than in women.[1]

This is consistent with the finding that leaderless groups have a natural tendency to elect self-centered, overconfident, and narcissistic individuals as leaders and that these personality characteristics are not equally common in men and women.[2] In line with this, Freud argued that the psychological process of leadership occurs because a group of people—the followers—have replaced their own narcissistic tendencies with those of the leader, such that their love for the leader is a disguised form of self-love or a substitute for their inability to love themselves. "Another person's narcissism," he said, "has a great attraction for those who have renounced part of their own . . . as if we envied them for maintaining a blissful state of mind."

The truth of the matter is that pretty much anywhere in the world, men tend to *think* that they are much smarter than women.[3] Yet arrogance and overconfidence are inversely related to leadership talent—the ability to build and maintain high-performing teams and to inspire followers to set aside their selfish agendas in order to work for the common interest of the group. Indeed, whether in sports, politics, or business, the best leaders are usually humble—and whether through nature or nurture, humility is a much more common feature in women than men. For example, women outperform men on emotional intelligence, which is a strong driver of modest behaviors.[4] Furthermore, a quantitative review of gender differences in personality involving more than 23,000 participants in 26 cultures indicated that women are more sensitive, considerate, and humble than men, which is arguably one of the least counter-intuitive findings in the social sciences.[5] An even clearer picture emerges when one examines the dark side of personality: For instance, our normative data, which includes thousands of managers from across all industry sectors and 40 countries, shows that men are consistently more arrogant, manipulative, and risk-prone than women.[6]

The paradoxical implication is that the same psychological characteristics that enable male managers to rise to the top of the corporate or political ladder are actually responsible for their downfall. In other words, what it takes to *get* the job is not just different from, but also the reverse of, what it takes to *do the job well*. As a result, too many incompetent people are promoted to management jobs, and promoted over more competent people.

Unsurprisingly, the mythical image of a "leader" embodies many of the characteristics commonly found in personality disorders, such as narcissism (Steve Jobs or Vladimir Putin), psychopathy (fill in the name of your favorite despot here), histrionic tendencies (Richard Branson or Steve Ballmer), or a Machiavellian personality (nearly any federal-level politician). The sad thing is not that these mythical figures are unrepresentative of the average manager, but that the average manager will fail precisely for having these characteristics.

In fact, most leaders—whether in politics or business—fail. That has always been the case: The majority of nations, companies, societies, and organizations are poorly managed, as indicated by their longevity, revenues, and approval ratings, or by the effects they have on their citizens, employees, subordinates, or members. Good leadership has always been the exception, not the norm.

So it struck me as a little odd that so much of the recent debate over getting women to "lean in" has focused on getting them to adopt more of these dysfunctional leadership traits. Yes, these are the people we often choose as our leaders—but should they be?

Most of the character traits that are truly advantageous for effective leadership are predominantly found in those who fail to impress others with their talent for management. This is especially true for women. There is now compelling scientific evidence supporting the notion that women are more likely to adopt more-effective leadership strategies than are men. Most notably, in a comprehensive review of studies, Alice Eagly and colleagues showed that female managers are more likely to elicit respect and pride from their followers, communicate their vision effectively, empower and mentor subordinates, and approach problem solving in a more flexible and creative way (all characteristics of "transformational leadership"), as well as fairly reward direct reports.[7] In contrast, male managers are statistically less likely to bond or connect with their subordinates, and they are relatively less adept at rewarding them for their actual performance. Although these findings may reflect a sampling bias that requires women to be more qualified and competent than men in order to be chosen as leaders, there is no way of really knowing until this bias is eliminated.

In sum, there is no denying that women's path to leadership positions is paved with many barriers, including a very thick glass ceiling. But a much bigger problem is the lack of career obstacles for incompetent men, and the fact that we tend to equate leadership with the very psychological features that make the average man a more inept leader than the average woman.[8] The result is a pathological system that rewards men for their incompetence while punishing women for their competence, to everybody's detriment.

TOMAS CHAMORRO-PREMUZIC is the Chief Talent Scientist at ManpowerGroup, a professor of business psychology at University College London and at Columbia University, and an associate at Harvard's Entrepreneurial Finance Lab. He's the author of *Why Do So Many Incompetent Men Become Leaders? (And How to Fix It)* (Harvard Business Review Press, 2019). Find him on Twitter @drtcp or at www .drtomascp.com.

Notes

1. Adrian Furnham et al., "Male Hubris and Female Humility? A Cross-Cultural Study of Ratings of Self, Parental, and Sibling Multiple Intelligence in America, Britain, and Japan," *Intelligence* 30, no. 1 (January–February 2001): 101–115; Amanda S. Shipman and Michael D. Mumford, "When Confidence Is Detrimental: Influence of Overconfidence on Leadership Effectiveness," *The Leadership Quarterly* 22, no. 4 (2011): 649–655; and Ernesto Reuben et al., "The Emergence of Male Leadership in Competitive Environments," *Journal of Economic Behavior & Organization* 83, no. 1 (June 2012): 111–117.

2. The Ohio State University, "Narcissistic People Most Likely to Emerge as Leaders," Newswise, October 7, 2008, https://newswise.com/articles/view/545089/.

3. Sophie von Stumm et al., "Decomposing Self-Estimates of Intelligence: Structure and Sex Differences Across

12 Nations," *British Journal of Psychology* 100, no. 2 (May 2009): 429–442.

4. S. Y. H. Hur et al., "Transformational Leadership as a Mediator Between Emotional Intelligence and Team Outcomes," *The Leadership Quarterly* 22, no. 4 (August 2011): 591–603.

5. Paul T. Costa, Jr., et al., "Gender Differences in Personality Traits Across Cultures: Robust and Surprising Findings," *Journal of Personality and Social Psychology* 81, no. 2 (2001): 322–331.

6. Blaine H. Gladdis and Jeff L. Foster, "Meta-Analysis of Dark Side Personality Characteristics and Critical Work Behaviors Among Leaders Across the Globe: Findings and Implications for Leadership Development and Executive Coaching," *Applied Psychology* 64, no. 1 (August 27, 2013).

7. Alice H. Eagly and Blair T. Johnson, "Gender and Leadership Style: A Meta-Analysis," *Psychological Bulletin* 108, no. 2 (1990), 233–256.

8. A. M. Koenig et al., "Are Leader Stereotypes Masculine? A Meta-Analysis of Three Research Paradigms," *Psychological Bulletin* 137, no. 4 (July 2011): 616–642.

Adapted from content posted on hbr.org,
August 22, 2013 (product #H00B50).

14

Less Confident People Are More Successful

By Tomas Chamorro-Premuzic

There is no bigger cliché in business psychology than the idea that high self-confidence is key to career success. It is time to debunk this myth. In fact, *low* self-confidence is more likely to make you successful.

After many years of researching and consulting on talent, I've come to the conclusion that self-confidence is only helpful when it's low. Sure, *extremely* low confidence is not helpful: It inhibits performance by inducing fear, worry, and stress, which may drive people to give up sooner or later. But just-low-enough confidence can help you recalibrate your goals so they are (a) more realistic and (b) attainable. Is that really a problem? Not everyone can be CEO of Coca-Cola or the next Steve Jobs.

If your confidence is low, rather than extremely low, you stand a better chance of succeeding than if you have high self-confidence. There are three main reasons for this:

Lower self-confidence makes you pay attention to negative feedback and be self-critical. Most people get trapped in their optimistic biases, so they tend to listen to positive feedback and ignore negative feedback. Although this may help them come across as confident to others, in any area of competence (e.g., education, business, sports, or performing arts) achievement is 10% performance and 90% preparation. Thus, the more aware you are of your soft spots and weaknesses, the better prepared you will be.

Low self-confidence may turn you into a pessimist, but when pessimism teams up with ambition it often produces outstanding performance. To be the very best at anything, you will need to be your own harshest critic, and that is almost impossible when your starting point is high self-confidence. Exceptional achievers always experience low levels of confidence and self-confidence, but they train hard and practice continually until they reach an acceptable level of competence. Indeed, success is the best medicine for your insecurities.

Lower self-confidence can motivate you to work harder and prepare more. If you are serious about your goals, you will have more incentive to work hard when you lack confidence in your abilities. In fact, low confidence is only demotivating when you are not serious about your goals.

Most people like the idea of being exceptional but not enough to do what it takes to achieve it. Most people want to be slim, healthy, attractive, and successful, but few people are willing to do what it takes to achieve it—which suggests that they don't really want these things as much as they think. As the legendary Paul Arden (former executive creative director at Saatchi & Saatchi) noted: "*I want* means: [I]f I want it enough I will get it. Getting what you want means making the decisions you need to make to get what you want." If you really want what you say you want, then your low confidence will only make you work harder to achieve it—because it will indicate a discrepancy between your desired goal and your current state.

Lower self-confidence reduces the chances of coming across as arrogant or being deluded. Although we live in a world that worships those who worship themselves—from Donald Trump to Lady Gaga to the latest reality TV "star"—the consequences of hubris are now beyond debate. According to Gallup, more than 60% of employees either dislike or hate their jobs, and the most common reason is that they have narcissistic bosses. If managers were less arrogant, fewer employees would be spending their working hours on Facebook, productivity rates would go up, and turnover rates would go down.

Lower self-confidence reduces the chances not only of coming across as arrogant but also of being deluded. Indeed, people with low self-confidence are more likely to admit their mistakes—instead of blaming others—and rarely take credit for others' accomplishments. This is arguably the most important benefit of low self-confidence because it points to the fact that low self-confidence can bring success, not just to individuals but also to organizations and society.

In brief, if you are serious about your goals, low self-confidence can be your biggest ally in achieving them. It will motivate you to work hard, help you work on your limitations, and stop you from being a jerk, deluded, or both. It is therefore time debunk the myth: High self-confidence isn't a blessing, and low self-confidence is not a curse—in fact, it is the other way around.

TOMAS CHAMORRO-PREMUZIC is the Chief Talent Scientist at ManpowerGroup, a professor of business psychology at University College London and at Columbia University, and an associate at Harvard's Entrepreneurial Finance Lab. He's the author of *Why Do So Many Incompetent Men Become Leaders? (And How to Fix It)* (Harvard Business Review Press, 2019). Find him on Twitter @drtcp or at www.drtomascp.com.

Adapted from content posted on hbr.org,
July 6, 2012 (product #H0092K).

Index